# Cooking with Herbs

**Your Promise of Success**

Welcome to the world of Confident Cooking, created for you in our test kitchen, where recipes are double-tested by our team of home economists to achieve a high standard of success.

MURDOCH BOOKS®
*Sydney • London • Vancouver • New York*

# HERBS AT A GLANCE

This chart will help you identify fresh herbs and tell you what they are best served with. We've used fresh rather than dried herbs throughout the book, unless indicated otherwise, because the flavour is far superior. As a general rule, however, you can substitute 1 teaspoon of dried herbs for 1 tablespoon of fresh herbs.

### BASIL

A fragrant green herb with a pungent taste, basil is a perfect partner for tomatoes and a staple in Italian cooking. The leaves bruise easily so they are best added just before serving. Apart from sweet basil, other varieties are purple or opal basil with deep red leaves, mint basil and Thai basil.

### CORIANDER

A light-green herb, which looks like flat-leaf parsley, but with lighter green leaves. Coriander has a fresh, peppery flavour and a unique aroma. The whole plant is eaten—the roots, stems, leaves and seeds. Used in Asian cooking, it goes well with seafood, curries and tomato salsa.

### CURRY LEAVES

Small, pointed green leaves with a spicy curry flavour. The leaves may be used fresh or dried and are usually chopped and fried in oil until crisp before adding other curry ingredients.

### DILL

A feathery, fern-like herb with a soft aniseed flavour and aroma. Cooking diminishes the flavour and colour—fold through just before serving. Dill is used with potatoes and other vegetables, and fish. It is an essential ingredient in pickled cucumbers.

## Bay Leaves

Dark glossy leaves of the bay tree with a strong spicy flavour. They are an essential ingredient in a bouquet garni. Used to flavour casseroles, soups, stews and marinades, the bay leaf is removed before serving.

## Chervil

A soft, delicate herb with a slightly sweet anise flavour, and leaves that resemble flat-leaf parsley. The flavour diminishes after chopping so it should be added near the end of cooking. Delicious in hollandaise sauces, creamy soups or tossed through salads.

## Chives

A thin, grass-like herb with a distinctive onion flavour. It is easier to snip chives using sharp kitchen scissors rather than a knife. Cooking reduces the flavour so add just before serving. Chives are a perfect accompaniment to eggs, creamy soups and fish.

## Fennel

Fine, feathery leaves with an aniseed flavour. Florence fennel is grown for the bulbous base, stalk and leaves. Use whole stalks and leaves on barbecued fish and pork, and the chopped fresh leaves in soups, dressings and to flavour vegetables.

## Garlic Chives

A flat, grass-like herb with a garlic and onion flavour, often used in Asian food. Cooking diminishes the flavour so add just before serving. Garlic chives are delicious with noodles, rice, soups or scrambled eggs.

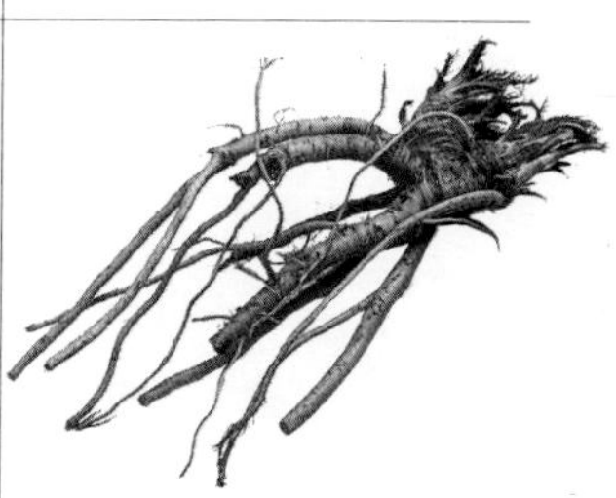

## Horseradish

A root of the mustard family with a pungent, biting flavour. Cooking diminishes the flavour so grate and use raw in dressings of cream and vinegar and serve with roast beef, smoked fish or potato salads.

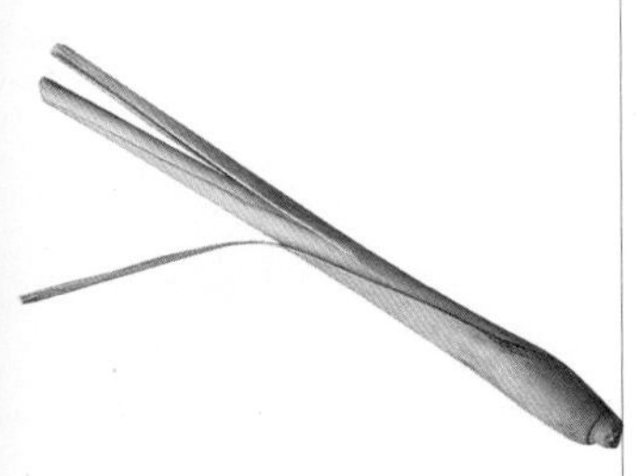

## Lemon Grass

A long, thick, grass-like plant with a strong lemon flavour. Finely chop or bruise the white part of the stalk. An essential ingredient in Asian cooking.

## Marjoram

Small, rounded green leaves, related to oregano but with a less strong taste. Cooking diminishes the flavours. Use the whole sprig or the chopped leaves in savoury pies, omelettes and stuffings.

## Mint

A dark-green herb with a strong, fresh flavour. There are many varieties, but spearmint is the most common. Mint is delicious with peas, potatoes, lamb roasts, salads, ice creams, sorbets, drinks and punches.

## Rosemary

A dark-green herb with soft, spiky leaves and a strong aroma and flavour. Use sparingly with potatoes and lamb, and in stuffings and marinades.

## Sage

A soft, green-grey long leaf with a strong, slightly bitter flavour. Used traditionally to temper rich, oily meats. Sage is delicious with poultry, game and pork, and in stuffings and creamy sauces.

## Sorrel

A large leafed herb resembling young English spinach, with a slightly sour taste and lemon aroma. Cooking diminishes the flavour and sorrel should not be prepared using aluminium utensils or it will discolour. Use with potatoes and in soups, marinades and omelettes.

## Oregano

Small, soft, pointed leaves with a strong aroma and flavour. Used in Italian and Greek dishes, oregano is delicious in tomato sauces and casseroles, and with vegetables, pizzas and salads. Use the chopped leaves as an ingredient or garnish.

## Parsley

A dark-green, curly leafed herb with a mild, crisp flavour. The chopped leaves can be used as a garnish or an ingredient. Use parsley in salads, egg dishes, pasta and mornays.

## Parsley
(Flat-leaf)

Also known as Italian or continental parsley. Flat-leafed, dark-green herb with a slightly more pungent flavour than curly parsley. Used in tabouli, it is also delicious with chicken, fish and vegetables.

## Tarragon

A thin-leafed, dark-green herb with a distinctive flavour and aroma. Traditionally used to flavour vinegar, it is widely used in French cuisine, namely hollandaise, Béarnaise and tartare sauce. Delicious in marinades, and with fish and poultry.

## Thyme

A fragrant, small-leafed herb. Thyme comes in a number of varieties, garden and lemon being the most common. Rub over veal or lamb before roasting, or use the leaves to flavour stuffings, herb bread, tomatoes or soups.

## Vietnamese Mint

The leaf of a creeping plant that grows throughout Asia. It is eaten raw in salads and has a sharp flavour that is similar to coriander. Use with chicken, fish or vegetables.

# Cooking with Herbs

Using fresh herbs to flavour food may not be a recent invention, but these recipes present some mouthwatering new ideas.

## Tomato and Basil Croustades

*Preparation time:* 30 minutes
*Total cooking time:* 20 minutes
*Serves 4*

*1 day-old unsliced white loaf*
*3 tablespoons olive oil*
*2 cloves garlic, crushed*
*3 tomatoes, diced*
*250 g (8 oz) bocconcini, cut into small chunks*
*1 tablespoon tiny capers, rinsed and dried*
*1 tablespoon extra virgin olive oil*
*2 teaspoons balsamic vinegar*
*1/3 cup (20 g/3/4 oz) shredded basil*

**1.** Preheat the oven to moderate 180°C (350°F/Gas 4). Remove the crusts from the bread and cut it into 4 even pieces. Using a small serrated knife, cut a square from the centre of each piece of bread, leaving a border of about 1.5 cm (5/8 inch) on each side. You should be left with 4 'boxes'. Combine the oil and garlic and brush all over the croustades. Place on a baking tray and bake for about 20 minutes, or until the croustades are golden and crisp. Be careful not to let them burn.

**2.** Meanwhile, combine the tomato and bocconcini with the tiny capers. Combine the oil and balsamic vinegar, drizzle over the tomato mixture and gently toss. Season with salt and freshly ground black pepper, and stir in the basil.

**3.** Spoon the tomato mixture into the croustades, allowing any excess to tumble over the sides.

NUTRITION PER SERVE: *Protein 30 g; Fat 40 g; Carbohydrate 80 g; Dietary Fibre 6 g; Cholesterol 40 mg; 3355 kJ (800 cal)*

*Tomato and Basil Croustades*

## Thai Beef Salad

*Preparation time:*
30 minutes
*Total cooking time:*
5 minutes
*Serves 6*

*2 tablespoons dried shrimp*
*1 tablespoon sesame oil*
*500 g (1 lb) rump steak*
*125 g (4 oz) English spinach, shredded*
*1 cup (90 g/3 oz) bean sprouts*
*1 red onion, sliced*
*1 small red capsicum, cut into thin strips*
*1 small cucumber, cut into thin strips*
*200 g (6 1/2 oz) daikon radish, cut into thin strips*
*1 small tomato, seeded and thinly sliced*
*1/2 cup (15 g/1/2 oz) coriander leaves*
*1/4 cup (5 g/1/4 oz) mint leaves*
*2 cloves garlic, chopped*
*2 red and 2 green chillies, chopped*

***Dressing***
*3 tablespoons lime juice*
*3 tablespoons fish sauce*
*1 tablespoon finely chopped lemon grass*
*1 teaspoon sugar*

**1.** Soak the dried shrimp in hot water for 15 minutes. Drain well and chop finely.
**2.** Heat the oil in a frying pan over high heat and cook the steak for 1 1/2–2 minutes on each side, or until medium rare. Allow the steak to cool, then slice thinly.
**3. To make Dressing:** Whisk together the lime juice, fish sauce, lemon grass and sugar.
**4.** Place the spinach on a serving plate and top with the shrimp, beef, vegetables, coriander, mint, garlic and chillies. Drizzle with the Dressing and serve.

NUTRITION PER SERVE:
*Protein 25 g; Fat 6 g; Carbohydrate 6 g; Dietary Fibre 3 g; Cholesterol 70 mg; 755 kJ (180 cal)*

## Nasturtium Salad

*Preparation time:*
20 minutes
*Total cooking time:*
Nil
*Serves 4–6*

*1 large green oak-leaf lettuce*
*8 young and tender nasturtium leaves*
*2 Lebanese cucumbers, finely sliced*
*1 green capsicum, finely sliced*
*1 celery stick, cut into julienne strips*
*4–6 young nasturtium flowers*

***Dressing***
*2 tablespoons olive oil*
*2 tablespoons sunflower oil*
*1 clove garlic, crushed*
*2 tablespoons cider vinegar*
*3 teaspoons honey*
*1 tablespoon finely chopped mint*

**1.** Tear the lettuce and nasturtium leaves into pieces and arrange on a salad platter. Scatter the cucumber slices, capsicum slices and celery over the leaves. Gently tear the nasturtium flowers into pieces, reserving a couple of whole flowers for decoration. Scatter the flower pieces over the salad.
**2. To make Dressing:** Combine the oils, garlic, vinegar and honey in a small bowl and whisk until well combined. Season with salt and black pepper, and stir in the mint.
**3.** Just before serving, drizzle the Dressing over the salad and garnish with the reserved flowers.

NUTRITION PER SERVE (6):
*Protein 2 g; Fat 15 g; Carbohydrate 5 g; Dietary Fibre 2 g; Cholesterol 0 mg; 615 kJ (145 cal)*

**Note:** Nasturtiums are one of the few edible flowers. Both the flowers and the leaves are edible.

*Thai Beef Salad (top) with Nasturtium Salad*

## Fennel and Chive Soufflés

*Preparation time:* 20 minutes
*Total cooking time:* 20 minutes
*Serves 4*

*2 tablespoons butter*
*1 clove garlic, crushed*
*2 tablespoons plain flour*
*1 cup (250 ml/8 fl oz) milk*
*4 eggs, separated, plus 2 egg whites*
*2 tablespoons chopped fennel fronds*
*1/2 cup (60 g/2 oz) grated Cheddar cheese*
*1/4 teaspoon grated nutmeg*
*1/4 cup (15 g/1/2 oz) chopped chives*

**1.** Preheat the oven to moderately hot 200°C (400°F/Gas 6). Grease four 1-cup (250 ml/8 fl oz) ramekins. Melt the butter in a pan, add the garlic and fry for 1 minute. Stir in the flour and continue cooking for 1 minute. Remove from the heat and whisk in the milk. Return to the heat and stir until thickened. Cover and leave to cool.
**2.** In a separate bowl, mix together the egg yolks, fennel, cheese and nutmeg. Season with salt and cracked black pepper, then set aside. Whisk the 6 egg whites in a dry bowl until stiff peaks form.
**3.** Combine the cooled sauce with the cheese mixture, then gently fold in the egg whites and chives. Spoon into the ramekins and bake for 15 minutes, or until the soufflés are puffed and golden.

NUTRITION PER SERVE: *Protein 15 g; Fat 20 g; Carbohydrate 8 g; Dietary Fibre 1 g; Cholesterol 230 mg; 1150 kJ (275 cal)*

**Note:** Avoid opening the oven while the soufflés are cooking.

## Herbed Eggplant with Tarragon Mayonnaise

*Preparation time:* 35 minutes
*Total cooking time:* 20 minutes
*Serves 2–4*

*2 eggplants, thinly sliced*
*2 sprigs fennel, chopped*
*1 small red chilli, seeded and finely chopped*
*4 sprigs thyme, chopped*
*1/3 cup (80 ml/2 3/4 fl oz) olive oil*
*1/4 teaspoon salt*

***Tarragon Mayonnaise***
*3 tablespoons good-quality mayonnaise*
*1/2 cup (125 g/4 oz) ricotta cheese*
*1 hard-boiled egg yolk, finely grated*
*juice and grated rind of half a lemon*
*2 tablespoons chopped tarragon*
*2 tablespoons chopped flat-leaf parsley*

**1.** Sprinkle the eggplant slices with salt and leave in a colander for 30 minutes, then rinse well and pat dry with paper towels.
**2. To make Tarragon Mayonnaise:** Beat the mayonnaise and ricotta together. Stir in the egg yolk, lemon juice and rind and herbs, cover and refrigerate.
**3.** Combine the fennel, chilli, thyme, olive oil and salt in a bowl. Brush the eggplant with the herb oil and place under a hot grill until golden. Turn over, brush with herb oil and grill the other side.
**4.** Drizzle the remaining herb oil over the grilled eggplant and serve warm with the chilled Tarragon Mayonnaise.

NUTRITION PER SERVE (4): *Protein 6 g; Fat 30 g; Carbohydrate 8 g; Dietary Fibre 5 g; Cholesterol 75 mg; 1325 kJ (315 cal)*

*Fennel and Chive Soufflés (top) with Herbed Eggplant with Tarragon Mayonnaise*

## Feta, Onion and Olive Herb Pie

*Preparation time:* 40 minutes
*Total cooking time:* 45 minutes
*Serves 4–6*

*2 teaspoons sugar*
*7 g (1/4 oz) dried yeast*
*2 tablespoons olive oil*
*1/2 cup (60 g/2 oz) plain flour*
*1 cup (125 g/4 oz) self-raising flour*
*1/2 teaspoon salt*
*1 onion, sliced*
*1/2 cup (15 g/1/2 oz) flat-leaf parsley, chopped*
*1 sprig rosemary, chopped*
*3 sprigs thyme, chopped*
*5 basil leaves, torn*
*1/4 cup (40 g/1 1/4 oz) pine nuts*
*1 clove garlic, crushed*
*175 g (5 3/4 oz) feta cheese, crumbled*
*1/4 cup (35 g/1 1/4 oz) olives, chopped*

**1.** Dissolve 1 teaspoon of the sugar in 1/2 cup (125 ml/4 fl oz) tepid water and sprinkle the yeast over the top. Leave for 10 minutes, or until frothy, then mix with 1 tablespoon of the oil. Sift the flours and salt into a large bowl. Make a well in the centre and pour in the yeast mixture. Mix well and knead on a floured board until smooth. Cut in half. Roll out to make two 20 cm (8 inch) circles. Cover with a cloth and put in a warm place for 10–15 minutes, or until doubled in size.
**2.** Preheat the oven to moderately hot 200°C (400°F/Gas 6). Heat the remaining oil in a frying pan and cook the onion for 10 minutes, or until golden brown. Sprinkle with the remaining sugar and cook until caramelised.
**3.** Transfer the onion to a bowl and mix with the herbs, pine nuts, garlic, cheese and olives. Spread on top of one of the bread circles. Dampen the edge with water and lay the second bread circle on top. Press the edges together to seal. Pinch the edges together to form a pattern and cut a few slits in the top to allow steam to escape during cooking. Bake for 30–35 minutes, or until crisp and golden brown. Serve warm.

NUTRITION PER SERVE (6): *Protein 10 g; Fat 20 g; Carbohydrate 25 g; Dietary Fibre 3 g; Cholesterol 20 mg; 1275 kJ (305 cal)*

*Feta, Onion and Olive Herb Pie (top) with Gremolata Chicken*

## Gremolata Chicken

*Preparation time:* 15 minutes
*Total cooking time:* 45 minutes
*Serves 4*

*1/3 cup (10 g/1/4 oz) chopped flat-leaf parsley*
*2 cloves garlic, finely chopped*
*3 teaspoons finely grated lemon rind*
*4 chicken marylands (chicken quarters)*
*olive oil, for brushing*
*lemon wedges, to serve*

**1.** Preheat the oven to moderately hot 200°C (400°F/Gas 6). Mix the parsley, garlic and lemon rind in a bowl and season with salt and pepper. Using your fingers, carefully loosen the skin from the chicken and fill with the parsley mixture. Pat the skin back to its original shape.
**2.** Put the chicken in a baking dish, brush lightly with the oil and bake for 45 minutes, or until the chicken juices run clear. Serve immediately with the lemon wedges.

NUTRITION PER SERVE: *Protein 30 g; Fat 25 g; Carbohydrate 1 g; Dietary Fibre 0 g; Cholesterol 140 mg; 1445 kJ (345 cal)*

## Fresh Spring Rolls with Lamb and Garlic Chives

*Preparation time:* 40 minutes
*Total cooking time:* 5 minutes
*Makes 6*

*2 lamb fillets*
*1/3 cup (40 g/1 1/4 oz) chopped garlic chives*
*2 tablespoons lemon juice*
*1/2 teaspoon coarsely ground black pepper*
*6 rice paper wrappers*
*1 cup (75 g/2 1/2 oz) shredded lettuce*
*1 small cucumber, seeded and thinly sliced lengthways*
*1/2 cup (10 g/1/4 oz) mint leaves*
*1/2 red onion, sliced*
*1 avocado, sliced*
*1/2 large red capsicum, cut into strips*
*200 g (6 1/2 oz) hummus, to serve*

**1.** Heat a little oil in a medium pan, add the lamb fillets and cook over high heat for 3 minutes, or until they are browned all over. Reduce the heat and add the garlic chives, lemon juice and pepper. Simmer until slightly reduced and season with salt. Remove from the heat and allow to cool slightly. Slice the lamb fillets into long thin strips, return to the pan and cover with the pan juices.

**2.** Have a large bowl filled with water near your work surface and work with one rice paper wrapper at a time. Dip a rice paper wrapper into the water and hold it under for about 30 seconds, or until it is soft and pliable (some rice papers may take longer to soften, but if the rice paper is held under for too long it will be too soft and will split when it is rolled).

**3.** Place the softened rice paper on the work surface. Lay some lamb strips across the centre of the rice paper and drizzle with some of the pan juices. Top with some lettuce, cucumber, mint, onion, avocado and capsicum strips. Roll up tightly, folding in the sides, and place on a serving plate. Repeat with the remaining rice paper, lamb, vegetables and mint. Serve the spring rolls, whole or halved, with the hummus.

NUTRITION PER ROLL: *Protein 15 g; Fat 15 g; Carbohydrate 75 g; Dietary Fibre 4 g; Cholesterol 15 mg; 2110 kJ (500 cal)*

**Note:** Use large rice paper wrappers which may be purchased from Asian food stores.

*Fresh Spring Rolls with Lamb and Garlic Chives*

*1 Add the chopped garlic chives to the browned lamb fillets.*

*2 Hold the rice paper under the water until it is soft and pliable.*

*3 Lay the avocado and capsicum strips over the lamb and vegetables.*

*4 Fold the sides of the wrappers over the lamb and vegetables and roll up tightly.*

## Oregano Parmesan Cornbread

*Preparation time:*
15 minutes
*Total cooking time:*
20 minutes
*Serves 6*

*1/2 cup (75 g/2 1/2 oz) cornmeal*
*3/4 cup (90 g/3 oz) plain flour*
*2 teaspoons baking powder*
*1/4 teaspoon salt*
*1/4 cup (25 g/3/4 oz) grated Parmesan*
*1 egg*
*150 ml (5 fl oz) milk*
*1/4 cup (7 g/1/4 oz) chopped oregano*
*60 g (2 oz) butter, melted and cooled*

**1.** Preheat the oven to moderately hot 200°C (400°F/Gas 6) and grease a 20 cm (8 inch) square tin.
**2.** Sift the cornmeal, flour, baking powder and salt together into a bowl and stir in the Parmesan. Whisk the egg and milk in a separate bowl and add the oregano and butter. Fold gently into the cornmeal mixture.
**3.** Spoon the mixture into the tin, smooth the top with the back of a spoon and bake for 20 minutes, or until golden. Cut into squares and serve the cornbread warm, drizzled with a little melted butter, or cold, spread with butter.

NUTRITION PER SERVE:
*Protein 7 g; Fat 10 g; Carbohydrate 25 g; Dietary Fibre 1 g; Cholesterol 65 mg; 940 kJ (225 cal)*

## Fennel and Tomato Soup

*Preparation time:*
20 minutes
*Total cooking time:*
20 minutes
*Serves 4*

*500 g (1 lb) fennel bulb*
*4 ripe tomatoes, halved*
*1 tablespoon olive oil*
*1 onion, chopped*
*1 tablespoon fennel seeds, crushed*
*4 cups (1 litre) vegetable stock*
*2 tablespoons tomato paste*
*1 tablespoon lemon juice*

***Camembert Wedges***
*4 pitta breads*
*200 g (6 1/2 oz) Camembert cheese, thinly sliced*
*seasoned pepper, to sprinkle*

**1.** Halve the fennel bulb, remove the core and any tough outer pieces, and reserve the green tops for garnishing. Chop the remaining bulb. Grate the tomatoes and discard the skin.
**2.** Heat the oil in a large pan. Add the onion, fennel and fennel seeds and cook until the onions are translucent. Add the tomato, stock and tomato paste to the pan and bring to the boil. Reduce the heat and simmer, uncovered, for 5 minutes. Season with salt and pepper and stir in the lemon juice. Serve sprinkled with sprigs of reserved fennel top and the Camembert Wedges.
**3. To make Camembert Wedges:** Split the pitta breads open and top one half with the Camembert. Sprinkle with a little seasoned pepper. Replace the tops, pressing firmly to stick them together, and cook under a hot grill until browned. Cut into wedges while still hot and serve immediately.

NUTRITION PER SERVE:
*Protein 20 g; Fat 20 g; Carbohydrate 55 g; Dietary Fibre 10 g; Cholesterol 45 mg; 2080 kJ (495 cal)*

**Note:** The Camembert will be easier to slice when it is cold.

*Oregano Parmesan Cornbread (top) with Fennel and Tomato Soup*

## Leek and Lemon Thyme Tart

*Preparation time:*
45 minutes + chilling
*Total cooking time:*
1 hour 25 minutes
*Serves 6*

***Pastry***
*1 cup (125 g/4 oz) plain flour*
*60 g (2 oz) butter*
*1 egg yolk*

*3 small leeks*
*60 g (2 oz) butter*
*2 teaspoons sugar*
*1/3 cup (50 g/1 3/4 oz) chopped sun-dried tomatoes*
*1 tablespoon lemon thyme leaves, plus a few extra to garnish*
*3 tablespoons cream*
*1 egg, lightly beaten*

**1. To make Pastry:** Sift the flour into a bowl and season well. Rub in the butter with your fingertips, until crumbly. Make a well in the centre, add the egg yolk and enough water to form a dough. Gather into a ball and wrap in plastic wrap. Chill for 30 minutes.
**2.** Quarter the leeks lengthways, then cut in half, keeping the layers intact. Heat the butter in a large heavy-based pan. Add the leeks in a single layer, cut-side-up, and enough water to just cover. Sprinkle with the sugar and season with salt and pepper. Bring to the boil, reduce the heat to low and simmer, without stirring, for 30 minutes, or until the leeks are tender and the liquid a sticky glaze.
**3.** Preheat the oven to hot 210°C (415°F/ Gas 6–7). Lightly grease a 20 cm (8 inch) loose-bottomed flan tin. Roll out the pastry between 2 sheets of baking paper to line the tin, trim the edges and prick the base all over. Line with baking paper, fill with dried beans or rice and bake for 10 minutes. Remove the paper and rice and bake for 8 minutes, or until lightly browned. Allow to cool.
**4.** Reduce the oven to 180° (350°F/Gas 4). Sprinkle the pastry with the tomatoes and lemon thyme. Pour in the combined cream and egg and top with the leeks and any pan juices. Bake for 30 minutes, or until brown. Garnish with lemon thyme and cool slightly before cutting.

NUTRITION PER SERVE: *Protein 5 g; Fat 25 g; Carbohydrate 20 g; Dietary Fibre 2 g; Cholesterol 125 mg; 1225 kJ (290 cal)*

## Marinated Olives

*Preparation time:*
10 minutes + overnight chilling
*Total cooking time:*
Nil
*Fills a 1 litre jar*

*300 g (10 oz) green olives*
*300 g (10 oz) black olives*
*3 cloves garlic, sliced*
*2 cups (500 ml/16 fl oz) white vinegar*
*4 thin slices lemon, halved*
*2 cups (500 ml/16 fl oz) olive oil*
*2 tablespoons chopped rosemary*
*2 tablespoons chopped thyme*

**1.** Mix the olives, garlic and vinegar together. Refrigerate overnight.
**2.** Drain the olives, discarding the garlic. Spoon the olives and lemon into a 4-cup (1 litre) sterilised jar. Pour in the oil and store in the refrigerator until ready to use.
**3.** Stir in the herbs and return to room temperature to serve.

NUTRITION PER 100 G: *Protein 1 g; Fat 30 g; Carbohydrate 1 g; Dietary Fibre 1 g; Cholesterol 0 mg; 1175 kJ (280 cal)*

*Leek and Lemon Thyme Tart (top) with Marinated Olives*

## Oregano and Prosciutto Pinwheels

*Preparation time:*
30 minutes + chilling
*Total cooking time:*
10 minutes
*Serves 6–8 as appetisers*

*1 red capsicum*
*1 green capsicum*
*1 yellow capsicum*
*125 g (4 oz) cream cheese, softened*
*1/4 cup (25 g/3/4 oz) grated Parmesan*
*2 spring onions, finely chopped*
*1/4 cup (7 g/1/4 oz) chopped oregano*
*3 teaspoons chopped capers*
*1 tablespoon chopped pine nuts*
*12 thin slices prosciutto*

**1.** Quarter the capsicums and remove the seeds and white membrane. Place, skin-side-up, under a hot grill until the skin blackens and blisters. Leave in a plastic bag until cool. Peel away the skin and pat dry with paper towels.
**2.** Combine the cream cheese, Parmesan, spring onion, oregano, capers and pine nuts.
**3.** Place the capsicum pieces on the prosciutto slices and trim the prosciutto to the same size. Remove the capsicum and spread some cheese mixture on the prosciutto. Top with the capsicum and spread with a little more cheese mixture. Roll up tightly from the short end. Cover and chill for 1 hour, or until firm. Slice into 1 cm (1/2 inch) rounds and serve on toothpicks.

NUTRITION PER SERVE (8): *Protein 15 g; Fat 25 g; Carbohydrate 2 g; Dietary Fibre 1 g; Cholesterol 65 mg; 1170 kJ (275 cal)*

## Barbecued Goats Cheese

*Preparation time:*
20 minutes
*Total cooking time:*
6 minutes
*Serves 8*

*200 g (6 1/2 oz) packaged vine leaves*
*3 teaspoons bottled green or pink peppercorns, drained and chopped*
*1 tablespoon chopped marjoram*
*3 x 100 g (3 1/4 oz) rounds soft goats cheese*
*rye bread, to serve*

**1.** Place the vine leaves in a heatproof bowl. Cover with hot water to rinse away the brine. Drain well and pat dry with paper towels.
**2.** Combine the chopped peppercorns and marjoram in a shallow bowl or plate. Toss the goats cheese in this mixture until the sides are reasonably well coated. Arrange a few vine leaves, shiny-side-down, on a work surface. Wrap up each goats cheese round in a few layers of vine leaves. This will prevent the cheese from overcooking and losing its shape.
**3.** Cook the cheese on a barbecue hot plate or under a hot grill for 3 minutes on each side, or until the outside leaves are charred. Transfer to a plate and allow to cool to room temperature. (The cheese is too soft to serve when hot, but it will become firm as it cools.) Use scissors to cut away the vine leaves and serve the cheese with the sliced rye bread.

NUTRITION PER SERVE: *Protein 10 g; Fat 10 g; Carbohydrate 20 g; Dietary Fibre 4 g; Cholesterol 25 mg; 880 kJ (210 cal)*

**Note:** Well-drained ricotta may be used instead of goats cheese.

*Oregano and Prosciutto Pinwheels (top) with Barbecued Goats Cheese*

## Grilled Baby Salmon with Dill Cream

*Preparation time:*
25 minutes
*Total cooking time:*
25 minutes
*Serves 4*

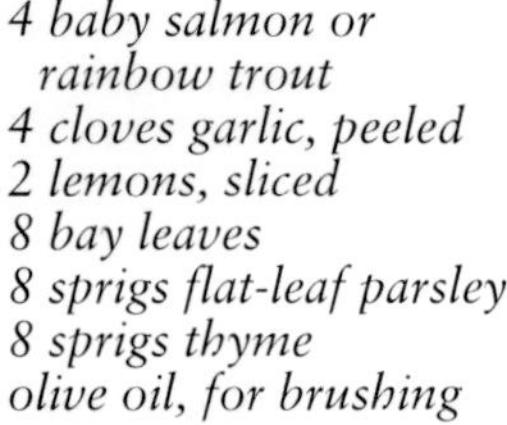

*4 baby salmon or rainbow trout*
*4 cloves garlic, peeled*
*2 lemons, sliced*
*8 bay leaves*
*8 sprigs flat-leaf parsley*
*8 sprigs thyme*
*olive oil, for brushing*

***Dill Cream***
*90 g (3 oz) butter*
*1 cup (250 ml/8 fl oz) fish stock*
*$1\frac{1}{2}$ teaspoons wholegrain mustard*
*1 cup (250 ml/8 fl oz) cream*
*juice of half a lemon*
*$\frac{1}{4}$ cup (15 g/$\frac{1}{2}$ oz) chopped dill*

**1.** Wash the salmon and pat them dry. Place a clove of garlic, a few slices of lemon and a bay leaf in the cavity of each fish. Divide the herb sprigs evenly into 8 bundles. Place a bundle of herbs on one side of each fish and tie them on with string, reserving the other 4 bundles. Brush the sides of the salmon with the olive oil.
**2. To make Dill Cream:** Melt the butter in a pan and add the fish stock, mustard and cream. Simmer for 15 minutes, or until the sauce is slightly thickened. Stir in the lemon juice and dill, and keep warm.
**3.** Cook the salmon on a preheated barbecue grill for 3–6 minutes on each side, or until cooked. Discard the herbs. Tie a fresh herb bundle with a bay leaf on each fish. Serve warm with Dill Cream.

NUTRITION PER SERVE:
*Protein 15 g; Fat 60 g; Carbohydrate 8 g; Dietary Fibre 5 g; Cholesterol 255 mg; 2600 kJ (620 cal)*

**Note:** If fish stock is not available, use half white wine and half water.

## Minted Green Bean Salad

*Preparation time:*
20 minutes
*Total cooking time:*
10 minutes
*Serves 4–6*

*500 g (1 lb) green beans*
*1 cup (200 g/$6\frac{1}{2}$ oz) freshly chopped tomatoes*
*$\frac{1}{4}$ cup (15 g/$\frac{1}{2}$ oz) torn mint*

***Dressing***
*$\frac{2}{3}$ cup (160 g/$5\frac{1}{4}$ oz) natural yoghurt*
*3 tablespoons cider vinegar*
*1 clove garlic, crushed*
*$\frac{1}{4}$ teaspoon salt*

**1.** Top and tail the green beans. Steam for 5–7 minutes, or until the beans are tender but still crisp. Once cooked, run under cold water to stop the cooking process. Drain and put in a serving bowl.
**2. To make Dressing:** Put the yoghurt, vinegar, garlic, salt and a little freshly ground black pepper in a screw-top jar and shake well until combined.
**3.** Spoon the tomato over the beans, drizzle with the Dressing and sprinkle with the mint.

NUTRITION PER SERVE (6):
*Protein 4 g; Fat 1 g; Carbohydrate 4 g; Dietary Fibre 3 g; Cholesterol 4 mg; 185 kJ (45 cal)*

**Note:** The edges of the mint will blacken once it is torn, so tear just before adding to the salad. There are many varieties of mint available. Try this recipe using apple mint or lemon mint.
**Variation:** Toss a few steamed sugar snap peas through the salad.

*Grilled Baby Salmon with Dill Cream (top) with Minted Green Bean Salad*

*1 Add the chives and the egg white to the prawns in a food processor.*

*2 Place the mixture on the wrappers and brush the edges with lightly beaten egg.*

## Prawn Ravioli with Basil Butter

*Preparation time:* 30 minutes + chilling
*Total cooking time:* 20 minutes
*Serves 4*

*500 g (1 lb) raw prawns, peeled and deveined*
*1 tablespoon chopped chives*
*1 egg white, lightly beaten*
*1 1/3 cups (350 ml/ 11 fl oz) cream*
*200 g (6 1/2 oz) packet won ton wrappers*
*1 egg, lightly beaten*

***Basil Butter***
*80 g (2 3/4 oz) butter*
*1 clove garlic, crushed*
*1/4 cup (15 g/1/2 oz) shredded basil*
*1/4 cup (40 g/1 1/4 oz) pine nuts*

**1.** Put the prawns in a food processor. Add the chives and egg white, and process until smooth. Season with salt and pepper. While the machine is running, gradually add the cream; do not over process. Transfer the mixture to a bowl, cover and refrigerate for 30 minutes.

**2.** Place 2–3 teaspoons of the prawn mixture on the centre of half the won ton wrappers. Brush the edges of the wrappers lightly with the beaten egg, and cover with the remaining wrappers. Press the edges firmly to seal. Using a 7 cm (2 3/4 inch) scone cutter, cut the ravioli into circles. Cook the ravioli in a large pan of boiling water for 4 minutes. (This is best done in batches to prevent overcrowding of the pan, which will cause the temperature to drop.) Drain the ravioli, taking care not to damage them, and divide among 4 warm serving plates.

**3. To make Basil Butter:** Melt the butter gently in a pan with the garlic. Add the shredded basil, pine nuts and a little freshly ground black pepper and cook until the butter turns a nutty brown colour. Drizzle the butter over the pasta and toss gently. Serve immediately.

NUTRITION PER SERVE: *Protein 30 g; Fat 65 g; Carbohydrate 15 g; Dietary Fibre 1 g; Cholesterol 400 mg; 3110 kJ (740 cal)*

**Note:** Gow gee wrappers may be used instead of the won ton wrappers. They are round so the ravioli do not have to be cut into circles. Buy them from Asian food stores.

*Prawn Ravioli with Basil Butter*

*3 Once the ravioli are sealed, cut into circles using a scone cutter.*

*4 Cook the basil butter until it turns a nutty brown colour.*

## Potatoes with Salami and Sage

*Preparation time:*
15 minutes
*Total cooking time:*
35 minutes
*Serves 4*

*2 potatoes, thickly sliced*
*350 g (11 1/4 oz) orange sweet potato, thickly sliced*
*125 g (4 oz) hot salami slices, cut into strips*
*1/4 cup (10 g/1/4 oz) sage leaves, shredded*
*2 cloves garlic, crushed*
*3 tablespoons olive oil*
*sage leaves, to serve*

**1.** Preheat the oven to very hot 230°C (450°F/Gas 8). Combine the potato and sweet potato slices with the salami, sage, garlic and oil in a bowl. Season with salt and pepper.
**2.** Spoon the potato mixture into a large baking dish and bake for 10 minutes. Reduce the heat to moderately hot 200°C (400°F/Gas 6) and bake for 20–25 minutes, or until the vegetables are crisp and tender. Sprinkle with the sage leaves.

NUTRITION PER SERVE: *Protein 9 g; Fat 25 g; Carbohydrate 15 g; Dietary Fibre 2 g; Cholesterol 30 mg; 1415 kJ (335 cal)*

## Roast Vegetables with Garlic and Thyme Purée

*Preparation time:*
30 minutes
*Total cooking time:*
1 hour 20 minutes
*Serves 2–4*

***Garlic and Thyme Purée***
*2 bulbs garlic*
*1 tablespoon thyme leaves*
*1 egg yolk*
*1/3 cup (80 ml/2 3/4 fl oz) olive oil*
*2 tablespoons lemon juice*

*1 eggplant, cut into 3 cm (1 1/4 inch) cubes*
*2 egg tomatoes, halved lengthways*
*2 zucchini, cut into 3 cm (1 1/4 inch) pieces*
*1 red capsicum, cut into chunks*
*1 yellow or green capsicum, cut into chunks*
*1 red onion, peeled and cut into 6–8 wedges*
*2 tablespoons extra virgin olive oil*

**1. To make Garlic and Thyme Purée:** Preheat the oven to moderately hot 200°C (400°F/Gas 6). Slice the tops off the bulbs of garlic and wrap the bulbs in foil. Bake for 1 hour, or until the garlic is soft.
**2.** While the garlic is cooking, place the vegetables on a baking tray and drizzle with the oil. Place in the oven with the garlic, on the highest shelf, 20 minutes before the garlic has finished cooking. Bake for 20 minutes. Remove the garlic and increase the oven to hot 220°C (425°F/Gas 7). Cook the vegetables for a further 20 minutes, or until they are tender inside with crispy edges, turning the eggplant once or twice.
**3.** Squeeze the garlic out of the skins and put in a food processor with the thyme leaves. While the motor is running, add the egg yolk and slowly pour in the oil. Add the lemon juice and season with sea salt and black pepper. Serve the purée with the vegetables.

NUTRITION PER SERVE (4): *Protein 4 g; Fat 30 g; Carbohydrate 6 g; Dietary Fibre 4 g; Cholesterol 45 mg; 1305 kJ (310 cal)*

**Note:** Try this with winter vegetables, such as parsnip, potato and pumpkin. Increase the cooking time slightly.

*Potatoes with Salami and Sage (top) with Roast Vegetables with Garlic and Thyme Purée*

## Thyme Pissaladière

*Preparation time:*
40 minutes
*Total cooking time:*
45 minutes
*Serves 4–6*

*1 teaspoon sugar*
*1 1/2 teaspoons dried yeast*
*3 tablespoons olive oil*
*1/2 cup (60 g/2 oz) plain flour*
*1 cup (125 g/4 oz) self-raising flour*
*1/2 teaspoon salt*
*2 onions, diced*
*3 large ripe tomatoes, chopped*
*2 tablespoons tomato paste*
*2 tablespoons chopped thyme*
*1/4 cup (25 g/3/4 oz) freshly grated Parmesan*
*80 g (2 3/4 oz) anchovies*
*15 black olives*

**1.** Dissolve the sugar in 1/2 cup (125 ml/4 fl oz) tepid water in a small bowl, and sprinkle with the yeast. When the yeast has turned frothy (after approximately 10 minutes) combine it with 1 tablespoon of the olive oil.
**2.** Sift together the flours and salt in a large bowl. Make a well in the centre and pour in the yeast mixture. Mix well and knead on a floured board until smooth (a little extra flour may be needed). Roll out to make a 23 cm (9 inch) circle. Place on a floured baking tray.
**3.** Preheat the oven to moderately hot 200°C (400°F/Gas 6). Heat the remaining oil in a frying pan. Add the onion, tomato, tomato paste and thyme, and cook for 20 minutes, or until all excess moisture has evaporated and a purée remains.
**4.** Spread the dough base with the vegetable purée and sprinkle with the grated Parmesan. Arrange the anchovies on top in a lattice pattern, placing one of the olives in each square. Bake for 20–25 minutes, or until the base is crisp.

NUTRITION PER SERVE (6): *Protein 8 g; Fat 15 g; Carbohydrate 15 g; Dietary Fibre 2 g; Cholesterol 15 mg; 950 kJ (225 cal)*

**Note:** If you find the taste of anchovies too strong, soak them in milk for 5 minutes, then drain and pat dry with paper towels. This bread dough base does not need to be set aside to rise.

*Thyme Pissaladière (top) with Marjoram Frittata*

## Marjoram Frittata

*Preparation time:*
20 minutes
*Total cooking time:*
20 minutes
*Serves 4–6*

*3 potatoes*
*6 eggs, lightly whisked*
*1/4 cup (7 g/1/4 oz) chopped marjoram*
*1 clove garlic, crushed*
*1/4 cup (25 g/3/4 oz) grated Parmesan*
*60 g (2 oz) butter*

**1.** Cook the potatoes in a pan of boiling water until they are just tender. Allow to cool slightly. Combine the eggs, marjoram, garlic and half the Parmesan in a bowl.
**2.** Cut the potatoes into 1 cm (1/2 inch) slices. Melt the butter in a frying pan and arrange the potato slices on the base of the pan. Pour in the egg mixture and sprinkle the remaining Parmesan over the top.
**3.** Cook over low heat for 7–10 minutes, or until the base is firm. Grill the top until it is golden and cooked through. Serve warm or at room temperature.

NUTRITION PER SERVE (6): *Protein 9 g; Fat 15 g; Carbohydrate 8 g; Dietary Fibre 1 g; Cholesterol 210 mg; 835 kJ (195 cal)*

## Thai Green Chicken Curry

*Preparation time:*
20 minutes
*Total cooking time:*
30 minutes
*Serves 4*

*90 g (3 oz) coriander leaves*
*1 stem lemon grass, white part only, chopped*
*1 tablespoon fish sauce*
*2 green chillies*
*2 teaspoons sesame oil*
*2 tablespoons oil*
*6 curry leaves*
*1 2/3 cups (410 ml/ 13 fl oz) coconut milk*
*500 g (1 lb) chicken thigh fillets, cut into thick strips*
*3 hard-boiled eggs, cut into quarters*
*coriander leaves, to garnish*

**1.** Put the coriander, lemon grass, fish sauce, chillies and sesame oil in a food processor. Process for 3 minutes, or until the mixture forms a smooth paste. Heat the remaining oil in a large pan, add the paste and curry leaves, and cook for 3 minutes, or until fragrant.
**2.** Pour in the coconut milk and 1 cup (250 ml/ 8 fl oz) water. Simmer gently for 10 minutes. Add the chicken and simmer for 10 minutes, or until tender.
**3.** Stir in the egg and cook for 3–4 minutes, or until heated through. Spoon onto a bed of steamed rice or noodles and garnish with the coriander leaves.

NUTRITION PER SERVE:
*Protein 35 g; Fat 40 g; Carbohydrate 3 g; Dietary Fibre 1 g; Cholesterol 240 mg; 2150 kJ (510 cal)*

## Mint and Spinach Rice

*Preparation time:*
20 minutes
*Total cooking time:*
25 minutes
*Serves 4*

*50 g (1 3/4 oz) butter*
*1 onion, finely chopped*
*3 cloves garlic, finely chopped*
*1 teaspoon cumin seeds*
*1 cup (200 g/6 1/2 oz) basmati rice, rinsed and drained*
*1 2/3 cups (410 ml/ 13 fl oz) chicken stock*
*4 cups (160 g/5 1/4 oz) roughly shredded English spinach leaves, or 1 packet (250 g/8 oz) frozen spinach, thawed, drained and chopped*
*1/4 cup (15 g/1/2 oz) chopped mint*

**1.** Melt the butter in a large pan. Add the onion and cook over moderate heat until it is soft and golden. Add the garlic and cumin seeds and cook for 1 minute.
**2.** Add the rice and stir until it is covered with the butter and onion mixture. Pour in the chicken stock. Bring to the boil; reduce the heat to very low and cover with a lid. Cook for 15 minutes, or until the rice is tender and most of the stock is absorbed. Take care not to let the rice burn. (If the rice runs out of stock to cook in, just add a little water.)
**3.** When the rice is cooked, remove the lid and stir in the shredded spinach, in batches. Keep stirring while the spinach cooks—this will only take a few minutes. Cook until any excess liquid has evaporated. Season well with salt and black pepper. Stir in the mint and serve immediately.

NUTRITION PER SERVE:
*Protein 5 g; Fat 10 g; Carbohydrate 40 g; Dietary Fibre 3 g; Cholesterol 30 mg, 1195 kJ (285 cal)*

**Note:** Cook the rice in water if chicken stock is not available.

*Thai Green Chicken Curry (top) with Mint and Spinach Rice*

## Thai Mussels

*Preparation time:*
15 minutes
*Total cooking time:*
15 minutes + standing
*Serves 4*

*1/3 cup (80 ml/ 2 3/4 fl oz) lime juice*
*1 tablespoon sweet chilli sauce*
*1 tablespoon palm or soft brown sugar*
*1 tablespoon fish sauce*
*1 tablespoon finely chopped lemon grass*
*2 tablespoons chopped coriander*
*1 finely chopped red chilli*
*1 kg (2 lb) fresh black mussels*

**1.** Mix together all of the ingredients except the mussels in a bowl. Leave for 10 minutes.
**2.** Place the mussels in a pan of simmering water and remove as the shells open. Discard any that do not open after 5 minutes. Use scissors to remove the mussels from the shells and serve immediately, in half shells with the sauce spooned over.

NUTRITION PER SERVE: *Protein 45 g; Fat 5 g; Carbohydrate 4 g; Dietary Fibre 0 g; Cholesterol 250 mg; 1010 kJ (240 cal)*

## Fresh Oysters with Tarragon

*Preparation time:*
15 minutes + 30 minutes marinating
*Total cooking time:*
Nil
*Serves 4*

***Vinaigrette***
*1 tablespoon chopped tarragon*
*2 teaspoons very finely chopped spring onion*
*2 teaspoons white wine vinegar*
*1 tablespoon lemon juice*
*2 tablespoons extra virgin olive oil*

*2 dozen oysters*

**1. To make Vinaigrette:** Whisk together the tarragon, spring onion, vinegar, lemon juice and olive oil.
**2.** Remove the oysters from their shells, keeping the shells. Mix the oysters with the vinaigrette; cover and chill for 30 minutes.
**3.** To serve, spoon the oysters back into their shells. Drizzle with any remaining vinaigrette.

NUTRITION PER SERVE: *Protein 4 g; Fat 10 g; Carbohydrate 0 g; Dietary Fibre 0 g; Cholesterol 25 mg; 470 kJ (110 cal)*

*Clockwise, from left: Thai Mussels; Fresh Oysters with Tarragon; Smoked Salmon in Dill Dressing*

## Smoked Salmon in Dill Dressing

*Preparation time:*
15 minutes
*Total cooking time:*
Nil
*Serves 4*

*400 g (12 3/4 oz) smoked salmon*

***Dill Dressing***
*2 tablespoons light olive oil*
*2 tablespoons sunflower oil*
*2 tablespoons lemon juice*
*3 teaspoons soft brown sugar*
*1/4 cup (15 g/1/2 oz) chopped dill*

**1.** Arrange the smoked salmon slices in a single layer, on individual plates or a large platter.
**2. To make Dressing:** Combine the oils, juice and sugar. Stir until the sugar dissolves. Season with salt and pepper. Mix in 2 tablespoons of the chopped dill.
**3.** Drizzle the dressing over the salmon. Using the back of a spoon, cover the salmon with the dressing. Sprinkle with the remaining dill and some black pepper.

NUTRITION PER SERVE: *Protein 25 g; Fat 25 g; Carbohydrate 2 g; Dietary Fibre 0 g; Cholesterol 50 mg; 1305 kJ (310 cal)*

# Chips and Breads

It's amazing what you can create with just a bunch of fresh herbs and some simple bread. These chips and breads are delightfully crisp and golden—try them with soups, salads or just as a tasty snack.

## Oregano Bagel Chips

Slice 4 day-old bagels into thin rings. Deep-fry in hot oil until the bagel rings are golden brown. Drain on paper towels and sprinkle with 2 tablespoons finely chopped oregano, a tiny pinch of chilli powder and a little salt. Serve warm with sweet chilli sauce or aioli.
*Serves 4*

NUTRITION PER SERVE: *Protein 10 g; Fat 35 g; Carbohydrate 45 g; Dietary Fibre 0 g; Cholesterol 0 mg; 2255 kJ (535 cal)*

**Note:** For low-fat chips, lightly spray each bagel ring with spray-on olive oil, sprinkle with the oregano, chilli and salt. Bake in a moderate 180°C (350°F/Gas 4) oven for 12 minutes, or until golden brown.

## Cheese and Herb Hot Bread

Preheat the oven to moderately hot 200°C (400°F/Gas 6). Mash 100 g ($3^1/4$ oz) softened butter with $^1/2$ cup (65 g/$2^1/4$ oz) finely grated Gruyère cheese, 2 tablespoons each parsley and chives, 1 tablespoon shredded basil and $^1/2$ teaspoon Dijon mustard.

Cut a French stick loaf diagonally into 2.5 cm (1 inch) slices, but don't cut quite to the bottom. Spread the cheese and herb butter on each side of the bread slices. Wrap the loaf in aluminium foil and bake for 20 minutes, or until the bread is hot and crisp and the butter and cheese are melted. *Serves 6*

NUTRITION PER SERVE: *Protein 9 g; Fat 20 g; Carbohydrate 30 g; Dietary Fibre 2 g; Cholesterol 55 mg; 1340 kJ (320 cal)*

## Lavash Bites

Preheat the oven to moderately hot 200°C (400°F/Gas 6). Brush 3 sheets lavash bread with 2 tablespoons oil. Using scissors, cut the bread into long thin triangles (they do not have to be the same size). Sprinkle with 1/3 cup (35 g/1 1/4 oz) freshly grated Parmesan and 3 tablespoons each of chopped flat-leaf parsley and shredded basil. Sprinkle lightly with sweet paprika. Bake for 10 minutes, or until the lavash bites are crisp and golden. *Serves 6*

NUTRITION PER SERVE: *Protein 8 g; Fat 10 g; Carbohydrate 35 g; Dietary Fibre 3 g; Cholesterol 6 mg; 1100 kJ (260 cal)*

*Left to right: Oregano Bagel Chips; Cheese and Herb Hot Bread; Lavash Bites*

## Fresh Herb Pakoras

*Preparation time:*
30 minutes + standing
*Total cooking time:*
10 minutes
*Makes 30*

*1 1/2 cups (165 g/ 5 1/2 oz) besan (chickpea flour)*
*1 1/2 teaspoons salt*
*1 teaspoon turmeric*
*1/2 teaspoon chilli powder*
*1 1/2 teaspoons garam masala*
*1 zucchini, diced*
*1 small orange sweet potato, diced*
*1/2 cup (60 g/2 oz) cauliflower florets*
*1/3 cup (50 g/1 3/4 oz) peas*
*1 small onion, diced*
*2 tablespoons chopped coriander*
*2 tablespoons chopped basil*
*2 tablespoons chopped parsley*
*2 cloves garlic, crushed*
*oil, for deep-frying*
*plain yoghurt and mango chutney, to serve*

**1.** Sift together the flour, salt, turmeric, chilli powder and garam masala. Beat in 1/2 cup (125 ml/4 fl oz) water until a stiff batter forms. Cover and leave for 30 minutes.
**2.** Beat the mixture again and stir in the vegetables, chopped herbs and garlic. Heat the oil until a cube of bread sizzles when dropped in. Drop heaped teaspoons of the mixture into the hot oil and cook until golden. Drain on paper towels before serving with plain yoghurt and mango chutney.

NUTRITION PER PAKORA:
*Protein 1 g; Fat 8 g; Carbohydrate 6 g; Dietary Fibre 1 g; Cholesterol 0 mg; 430 kJ (100 cal)*

*Fresh Herb Pakoras (top) with Crab Cakes with Avocado Salsa*

## Crab Cakes with Avocado Salsa

*Preparation time:*
15 minutes + chilling
*Total cooking time:*
6 minutes
*Serves 4*

*2 eggs*
*340 g (10 3/4 oz) can crab meat, drained*
*1 tablespoon chopped spring onion*
*1 tablespoon mayonnaise*
*2 teaspoons sweet chilli sauce*
*1 1/4 cups (100 g/ 3 1/4 oz) fresh white breadcrumbs*
*oil, for shallow-frying*

*Avocado Salsa*
*2 ripe egg tomatoes, chopped*
*1 small red onion, finely chopped*
*1 large avocado, diced*
*3 tablespoons lime juice*
*2 tablespoons chervil leaves*
*1 teaspoon caster sugar*

**1.** Beat the eggs lightly in a bowl. Add the crab meat, chopped spring onion, mayonnaise, sweet chilli sauce and fresh breadcrumbs, and stir well to combine. Season to taste with salt and freshly ground black pepper. Cover the mixture and refrigerate for 30 minutes.
**2. To make Avocado Salsa:** Put the tomato, onion, avocado, lime juice, chervil leaves and sugar in a medium bowl. Season with salt and pepper, and toss gently to combine.
**3.** Using wet hands, form the crab mixture into 8 small flat cakes. Heat the oil in a large heavy-based pan and cook the crab cakes over medium heat for about 6 minutes, or until golden brown on both sides. Drain well on paper towels and serve immediately with the Avocado Salsa.

NUTRITION PER SERVE:
*Protein 20 g; Fat 45 g; Carbohydrate 40 g; Dietary Fibre 10 g; Cholesterol 75 mg; 2780 kJ (660 cal)*

## Cauliflower, Cheese and Chive Soup

*Preparation time:*
15 minutes
*Total cooking time:*
25 minutes
*Serves 4*

*30 g (1 oz) butter*
*3/4 cup (100 g/3 1/4 oz) chopped leek*
*750 g (1 1/2 lb) cauliflower, chopped*
*2 1/2 cups (600 ml/20 fl oz) milk*
*2 cups (500 ml/16 fl oz) chicken stock*
*1 cup (125 g/4 oz) grated Cheddar cheese*
*2 tablespoons chopped chives*

**1.** Melt the butter in a large pan. Add the leek and stir over medium heat for 3 minutes, or until soft. Add the cauliflower, milk and stock, and bring to the boil. Reduce the heat, cover and simmer for 15 minutes, or until the cauliflower is tender. Set aside to cool.
**2.** Process the mixture in batches in a food processor or blender, until smooth. Return to the cleaned pan and heat without boiling.
**3.** Stir in the cheese until it melts. Season the soup with salt and pepper and add the chives. Garnish with some extra chives and serve immediately.

NUTRITION PER SERVE:
*Protein 20 g; Fat 25 g; Carbohydrate 15 g; Dietary Fibre 4 g; Cholesterol 70 mg; 1380 kJ (330 cal)*

## Veal Casserole with Bacon and Bay Leaves

*Preparation time:*
20 minutes
*Total cooking time:*
1 hour 30 minutes
*Serves 4*

*4 veal chops*
*1/4 cup (30 g/1 oz) plain flour*
*2 tablespoons oil*
*2 onions, sliced*
*2 cloves garlic, crushed*
*1/2 cup (125 ml/4 fl oz) dry red wine*
*1/2 cup (125 ml/4 fl oz) chicken stock*
*2 juniper berries*
*4 bay leaves*
*2 ripe tomatoes, finely chopped*
*2 bacon rashers, cut into wide strips*

**1.** Preheat the oven to moderate 180°C (350°F/Gas 4). Trim any excess fat from the veal chops. Toss the chops in the flour, shaking off any excess. Heat the oil in a flameproof casserole dish with a lid (a pyrex dish would be best for this) that fits the chops in a single layer. Cook the chops until they are browned all over. Drain on paper towels.
**2.** Add the onion and garlic to the dish and stir over the heat until the onion is translucent. Pour in the wine and simmer until the liquid is reduced by half, then add the stock, berries and bay leaves. To extract the best aroma from the bay leaves, fold them along the centre vein.
**3.** Return the veal chops to the dish, top with the tomato and bacon, and season with salt and pepper. Cover and bake for 1 hour, or until the veal is tender.

NUTRITION PER SERVE:
*Protein 25 g; Fat 15 g; Carbohydrate 9 g; Dietary Fibre 2 g; Cholesterol 85 mg; 1280 kJ (305 cal)*

**Note:** If you don't have a pyrex dish, do steps 1–3 in a frying pan, then transfer the mixture to an ovenproof dish, cover with foil and bake for 1 hour, or until tender.
**Variation:** Lamb chops may be substituted for the veal.

*Cauliflower, Cheese and Chive Soup (top) with Veal Casserole with Bacon and Bay Leaves*

## Olive Basil Cheese Spread

*Preparation time:*
15 minutes
*Total cooking time:*
Nil
*Serves 8–10*

*250 g (8 oz) softened cream cheese*
*200 g (6 1/2 oz) feta cheese*
*1/3 cup (20 g/3/4 oz) basil leaves*
*1/4 teaspoon cracked black pepper*
*3 tablespoons olive oil*
*15 Kalamata olives, pitted and roughly chopped*

**1.** Combine the cream cheese, feta cheese, basil, pepper and 1 tablespoon of the oil in a food processor. Process until well combined and smooth.
**2.** Fold in the olives and spoon into a serving bowl. Smooth the top with the back of the spoon. Pour the remaining oil over the top. Garnish with a little more cracked pepper and serve on warm bruschetta.

NUTRITION PER SERVE (10): *Protein 6 g; Fat 20 g; Carbohydrate 1 g; Dietary Fibre 0 g; Cholesterol 40 mg; 825 kJ (195 cal)*

## Smoked Salmon Pâté with Chive Pikelets

*Preparation time:*
30 minutes + standing
*Total cooking time:*
40 minutes
*Makes about 30*

*125 g (4 oz) smoked salmon*
*10 g (1/4 oz) butter*
*1 small onion, chopped*
*1 1/2 teaspoons horseradish cream*
*30 g (1 oz) soft butter, extra*
*3 teaspoons chopped tarragon*
*1 lime, cut into small triangles*
*red or black lumpfish caviar, to garnish*

***Chive Pikelets***
*1/2 cup (60 g/2 oz) self-raising flour*
*1 tablespoon coarsely chopped chives*
*1 egg yolk, lightly beaten*
*1/2 cup (125 ml/4 fl oz) milk*

**1.** Roughly chop the smoked salmon.
**2.** Heat the butter in a small pan, add the onion and cook until soft. Put the smoked salmon, onion, horseradish cream and extra butter in a food processor. Season with salt and freshly ground black pepper and process until the mixture is smooth. Add the tarragon and process until the pâté is just combined.
**3. To make Chive Pikelets:** Sift the flour with a pinch of salt in a small bowl. Add the chives and mix well. Make a well in the centre and add the yolk and enough milk to form a smooth, creamy batter, the consistency of thick cream. You can make the pikelets straight away, or allow the batter to stand for 15 minutes so the pikelets are more tender. Lightly grease a non-stick frying pan and drop teaspoons of the batter into the pan. When bubbles appear on the surface of the pikelet, turn it over and brown the other side. Transfer to a wire rack to cool. Repeat with the remaining batter.
**4.** Pipe or spread the pâté onto the pikelets, garnish with a slice of lime and some caviar. The pikelets may be assembled up to 3 hours ahead, covered and refrigerated.

NUTRITION PER PIKELET: *Protein 2 g; Fat 2 g; Carbohydrate 2 g; Dietary Fibre 0 g; Cholesterol 20 mg; 140 kJ (35 cal)*

*Olive Basil Cheese Spread (top) with Smoked Salmon Pâté with Chive Pikelets*

## Tuna with Sorrel Hollandaise

*Preparation time:*
15 minutes
*Total cooking time:*
10 minutes
*Serves 4*

*4 tuna steaks (about 150 g/5 oz each)*
*2 tablespoons olive oil*

***Sorrel Hollandaise***
*15 young sorrel leaves, stems removed*
*150 g (5 oz) butter*
*3 egg yolks*
*1 tablespoon lemon juice*

**1.** Brush the tuna steaks lightly with the olive oil. Cook in a frying pan for 2–3 minutes on each side, or until the tuna is cooked. Remove from the pan, cover and keep warm.
**2. To make Sorrel Hollandaise:** Cover the sorrel leaves with boiling water, drain and rinse in cold water. Pat the leaves dry with paper towels and chop them roughly. Melt the butter in a small pan. Put the egg yolks in a food processor and process for 20 seconds. With the motor running, add the hot butter in a thin steady stream and process until thick and creamy. Add the lemon juice and sorrel, and season with salt and black pepper. Process for a further 20 seconds.
**3.** Spoon the Sorrel Hollandaise over the warm tuna steaks on individual plates and serve immediately.

NUTRITION PER SERVE:
*Protein 40 g; Fat 50 g; Carbohydrate 0 g; Dietary Fibre 0 g; Cholesterol 310 mg; 2465 kJ (585 cal)*

## Black-eyed Bean Salad

*Preparation time:*
20 minutes + overnight soaking
*Total cooking time:*
35 minutes
*Serves 4*

*3/4 cup (150 g/5 oz) dried black-eyed beans*
*1 tablespoon balsamic vinegar*
*3 tablespoons olive oil*
*1/2 teaspoon sugar*
*1/2 red onion, diced*
*3 ripe tomatoes, diced*
*2 tablespoons chopped thyme*
*2 tablespoons chopped mint*
*2 tablespoons chopped basil*
*35 g (1 1/4 oz) rocket leaves*

**1.** Put the black-eyed beans in a large bowl. Cover with water and leave to soak overnight. Drain, put in a pan and cover with water. Cook for 15 minutes, then drain. Cover with fresh water, bring to the boil and simmer for 20 minutes, or until the beans are tender.
**2.** Drain the beans and season with salt and freshly ground black pepper. Add the balsamic vinegar, oil, sugar and onion. Cover and set aside to cool. Add the tomato, thyme, mint and basil, and toss gently to combine.
**3.** Arrange the salad on a bed of rocket leaves to serve.

NUTRITION PER SERVE:
*Protein 10 g; Fat 15 g; Carbohydrate 15 g; Dietary Fibre 9 g; Cholesterol 0 mg; 1035 kJ (245 cal)*

**Note:** For a better flavour prepare the beans a day in advance. Toss in the seasoning, vinegar, oil, sugar, onion and refrigerate overnight. Do not salt the beans until they are cooked. Salt in the water stops the beans absorbing liquid.
**Variation:** Any beans may be used, such as chickpeas, borlotti or red kidney beans.

*Tuna with Sorrel Hollandaise (top) with Black-eyed Bean Salad*

1 *Stir the rice into the butter and onion mixture until it is partly translucent.*

2 *Add a ladleful of the simmering stock and wine to the rice.*

## Herb Risotto

*Preparation time:*
20 minutes
*Total cooking time:*
30 minutes
*Serves 4*

*6–7 cups (1.5–1.75 litres) chicken stock*
*1/2 cup (125 ml/4 fl oz) white wine*
*50 g (1 3/4 oz) butter*
*1 onion, sliced*
*2 cloves garlic, chopped*
*2 cups (440 g/14 oz) arborio rice*
*1/4 cup (15 g/1/2 oz) chopped parsley*
*1/4 cup (15 g/1/2 oz) chopped chives*
*1/4 cup (15 g/1/2 oz) shredded basil*
*2 teaspoons thyme leaves*
*2 teaspoons rosemary*
*3/4 cup (75 g/2 1/2 oz) grated Parmesan*
*extra herbs, to garnish*

**1.** Pour the stock and wine into a pan and bring just to the boil. Reduce the heat to low and leave the stock at simmering point. Melt the butter in a large pan and add the onion. Cook over medium heat until the onion is soft and transparent. Add the garlic and cook for 1 minute.

**2.** Add the rice and stir until it is coated with the butter and is partly translucent. (This separates the grains of rice and ensures a creamy consistency.)

**3.** Lower the heat and slowly add the simmering stock, a ladleful at a time, stirring constantly. Maintain the heat so that the risotto cooks at a gentle simmer and only add the next ladle of stock when the liquid in the risotto is fully absorbed. After 20 minutes of cooking, add the herbs, then continue adding the stock and stirring for another 8 minutes. By this time the rice should be cooked and have a creamy consistency; however, taste the rice in order to check. If the rice is not cooked, add a little extra stock and continue cooking until the rice is tender. Add a final ladle of stock, stir in the Parmesan and season with salt and black pepper. Serve in warmed bowls and garnish with the herbs.

NUTRITION PER SERVE:
*Protein 15 g; Fat 15 g; Carbohydrate 85 g; Dietary Fibre 4 g; Cholesterol 50 mg; 2410 kJ (570 cal)*

**Note:** The risotto will thicken on standing as it continues to absorb the liquid. It should be served straight after the grated Parmesan is added or the risotto will be gluggy.

*Herb Risotto*

*3 Add the chopped herbs to the rice after 20 minutes of cooking.*

*4 Add a final ladleful of stock and stir in the grated Parmesan.*

## Chicken Herb Terrine

*Preparation time:* 25 minutes
*Total cooking time:* 1 hour 20 minutes
*Serves 6*

*10 slices prosciutto*
*1 onion, finely diced*
*1–2 cloves garlic, crushed*
*1 egg, lightly whisked*
*500 g (1 lb) chicken mince*
*500 g (1 lb) English spinach, steamed and chopped*
*1 tablespoon chopped thyme*
*1 tablespoon marjoram*
*2 tablespoons chopped parsley*

**1.** Preheat the oven to moderate 180°C (350°F/Gas 4). Line an 11 x 21 cm (4½ x 8½ inch) terrine dish or loaf tin with the prosciutto, overhanging the edge of the dish (to cover the terrine later).
**2.** Combine the onion, garlic, egg, chicken mince, spinach, thyme, marjoram and parsley in a large bowl. Season with ground black pepper and salt, and mix well. Spoon into the terrine dish and press down. Fold the prosciutto over the top. Cover well with foil.
**3.** Put the terrine in a baking dish and pour in enough warm water to come half-way up the sides of the terrine dish. Bake the terrine for 1 hour 20 minutes. Allow to cool, then drain off any excess liquid. Invert the terrine onto a board, cut into slices and serve warm or cold.

NUTRITION PER SERVE: *Protein 30 g; Fat 25 g; Carbohydrate 2 g; Dietary Fibre 3 g; Cholesterol 140 mg; 1450 kJ (345 cal)*

**Note:** Frozen spinach may be used in this recipe instead of fresh spinach. When using cooked or frozen spinach, squeeze out as much water as possible.

## Minted Rice and Grape Salad

*Preparation time:* 45 minutes
*Total cooking time:* 15 minutes
*Serves 4–6*

***Dressing***
*1/3 cup (80 ml/ 2 3/4 fl oz) olive oil*
*2 tablespoons red wine vinegar*
*1 teaspoon Dijon mustard*

*1 cup (185 g/6 oz) cooked brown rice (see Note)*
*1 cup (150 g/5 oz) cooked wild rice (see Note)*
*1 small red onion, diced*
*20 purple grapes, halved*
*20 green grapes, halved*
*1 cup (125 g/4 oz) chopped celery*
*1/4 cup (30 g/1 oz) chopped pecans*
*1/4 cup (15 g/½ oz) chopped mint*

**1. To make Dressing:** Mix the oil, vinegar and mustard in a screw-top jar. Season with salt and pepper, and shake well.
**2.** Combine the warm brown and wild rice in a large bowl. Pour in the Dressing. Cover and refrigerate to cool.
**3.** Add the onion, grapes, celery, pecans and mint to the rice. Toss gently and serve.

NUTRITION PER SERVE (6): *Protein 3 g; Fat 15 g; Carbohydrate 25 g; Dietary Fibre 2 g; Cholesterol 0 mg; 1085 kJ (260 cal)*

**Note:** You will need ½ cup (110 g/3 3/4 oz) raw brown rice and and ½ cup (95 g/ 3 1/4 oz) raw wild rice to yield 1 cup of cooked rice.

*Chicken Herb Terrine (top) with Minted Rice and Grape Salad*

## Asian Mushroom Ragout

*Preparation time:*
20 minutes
*Total cooking time:*
10 minutes
*Serves 4*

*1/3 cup (80 ml/ 2 3/4 fl oz) peanut oil*
*1 teaspoon sesame oil*
*2 cloves garlic, crushed*
*1 tablespoon grated fresh ginger*
*750 g (1 1/2 lb) mixed mushrooms, chopped (see Note)*
*2 tablespoons chopped coriander*
*1/2 teaspoon five spice powder*
*1/3 cup (80 ml/ 2 3/4 fl oz) beef stock*
*2 tablespoons sweet sherry*
*3 teaspoons soy sauce*
*375 g (12 oz) 2-minute noodles*

**1.** Place the oils in a medium pan, add the garlic and ginger and cook over low heat for 30 seconds. Add the mushrooms, coriander, five spice, stock, sherry and soy and cook, covered, over moderate heat for 5 minutes, stirring occasionally.
**2.** Cook the noodles in a large pan of boiling salted water until tender, then drain. Spoon the mushrooms over the hot noodles and serve immediately.

NUTRITION PER SERVE:
*Protein 15 g; Fat 30 g; Carbohydrate 20 g; Dietary Fibre 6 g; Cholesterol 45 mg; 1710 kJ (405 cal)*

**Note:** Try mushrooms such as Swiss brown, enoki, shiitake and oyster mushrooms.

## Beef Salad with Purple Basil Aïoli

*Preparation time:*
20 minutes
*Total cooking time:*
12 minutes
*Serves 4*

*500 g (1 lb/16 oz) rump steak, in one piece*
*2 tablespoons olive oil*
*250 g (8 oz) button mushrooms, sliced*
*2 teaspoons lemon juice*
*2 teaspoons chopped flat-leaf parsley*

***Purple Basil Aïoli***
*2 egg yolks*
*2 cloves garlic, crushed*
*1/2 cup (125 ml/4 fl oz) light olive oil*
*3 tablespoons extra virgin olive oil*
*1 tablespoon lemon juice*
*2 tablespoons chopped purple basil*

**1.** Brush the steak lightly with 2 teaspoons of the oil and cook under a hot grill or in a ribbed pan for 3–4 minutes on each side. Leave to cool completely before slicing the steak thinly. (The meat should be medium-rare.)
**2. To make Purple Basil Aïoli:** Put the egg yolks and garlic in a food processor and process until smooth. With the motor running, gradually add the oils in a thin stream, processing until thick. Add the lemon juice and 1 tablespoon of boiling water, and process until smooth. Season with salt and black pepper, and stir in the purple basil.
**3.** Heat the remaining oil in a pan, add the sliced mushrooms and stir over high heat until they are just soft. Remove from the heat, add the lemon juice and parsley, and season with salt and pepper. Leave to cool. Spoon the mushrooms onto a serving dish, top with the beef and the aïoli. Serve immediately.

NUTRITION PER SERVE:
*Protein 35 g; Fat 30 g; Carbohydrate 1 g; Dietary Fibre 2 g; Cholesterol 175 mg; 1730 kJ (410 cal)*

**Note:** Use green basil if purple is not available.

*Asian Mushroom Ragout (top) with Beef Salad with Purple Basil Aïoli*

## Herb Omelette

*Preparation time:*
10 minutes
*Total cooking time:*
5 minutes
*Serves 2*

*4 eggs*
*1 tablespoon chopped parsley*
*1 tablespoon chopped chives*
*2 tablespoons chopped sorrel*
*25 g (3/4 oz) butter*
*1/3 cup (40 g/1 1/4 oz) grated Gruyère cheese*

**1.** Break the eggs into a large bowl and beat with a fork until frothy. Add 2 tablespoons of water and the parsley, chives and sorrel. Season with salt and black pepper.
**2.** Heat a 20 cm (8 inch) heavy-based non-stick frying pan and add the butter. When the butter is foaming, swirl it around to cover the base of the pan. Pour in the egg and herb mixture and leave for a few seconds to allow the egg to set a little.
**3.** When the mixture is half cooked, sprinkle the omelette with the grated cheese. Allow the omelette to cook a little more (the base should be golden brown and the inside nearly set). Using an egg slice, fold one half of the omelette over the other. Flip it over onto a warm serving plate and serve immediately.

NUTRITION PER SERVE:
*Protein 20 g; Fat 25 g; Carbohydrate 0 g; Dietary Fibre 0 g; Cholesterol 410 mg; 1295 kJ (310 cal)*

## Potato and Horseradish Salad

*Preparation time:*
20 minutes
*Total cooking time:*
15 minutes
*Serves 4–6*

*1 kg (2 lb) new potatoes, peeled*
*freshly grated Parmesan and chopped parsley, to garnish*

***Dressing***
*1/2 cup (125 g/4 oz) sour cream*
*1/2 cup (125 ml/4 fl oz) olive oil*
*1 tablespoon lemon juice*
*1 tablespoon grated horseradish*
*1 red onion, finely sliced*
*1/4 cup (30 g/1 oz) black olives, pitted*
*2 tablespoons chopped chives*
*1/2 teaspoon salt*

**1.** Cook the potatoes in boiling water until they are just tender. Allow them to cool before roughly chopping them into chunks.
**2. To make Dressing:** Put the sour cream in a food processor. With the motor running, slowly add the oil in a thin steady stream and process until combined. Add the lemon juice, horseradish, onion, olives, chives, salt and a little freshly ground black pepper, and process in short bursts.
**3.** Pour the Dressing over the cooked potato, toss gently and spoon into a serving bowl. Garnish with the freshly grated Parmesan and chopped parsley.

NUTRITION PER SERVE (6):
*Protein 8 g; Fat 35 g; Carbohydrate 25 g; Dietary Fibre 3 g; Cholesterol 40 mg; 1790 kJ (425 cal)*

**Note:** If fresh horseradish is not available use 1–2 tablespoons of hot horseradish sauce instead. Sautéed bacon or mashed anchovies may also be added to the dressing.
**Variation:** 1 tablespoon of either Dijon or wholegrain mustard may be used instead of the grated horseradish.

*Herb Omelette (top) with Potato and Horseradish Salad*

## Capsicum Herb Rice Cake

*Preparation time:*
35 minutes
*Total cooking time:*
1 hour 20 minutes
*Serves 4*

*2 small red capsicums*
*olive oil, for brushing*
*1 cup (220 g/7 oz) short-grain rice*
*1 teaspoon salt*
*60 g (2 oz) butter, melted*
*3 spring onions, finely chopped*
*2 sprigs parsley, chopped*
*2 sprigs thyme, chopped*
*1 clove garlic, crushed*
*1 cup (125 g/4 oz) grated Cheddar cheese*
*1 egg, lightly beaten*
*1/2 cup (125 ml/4 fl oz) milk*

**1.** Preheat the oven to moderately hot 200°C (400°F/Gas 6) and lightly grease a 20 cm (8 inch) round baking dish. Brush the capsicums lightly with the olive oil and bake for 20 minutes, or until the skin blackens and blisters. Leave to cool under a tea towel or in a plastic bag.
**2.** Reduce the oven temperature to moderate 180°C (350°F/Gas 4). Put the rice, salt and 2 cups (500 ml/16 fl oz) water in a medium pan. Bring to the boil, cover and reduce the heat to the lowest setting. Cook for 15 minutes, or until the rice is tender. Remove from the heat and gently fluff the rice with a fork to separate the grains.
**3.** Peel the skin off the capsicums and discard with the core and seeds. Slice the flesh into thin strips. Put the capsicum strips in a large bowl with the cooked rice, melted butter, chopped spring onion, parsley, thyme, crushed garlic, grated cheese, egg and milk. Stir until the mixture is well blended.
**4.** Spoon the capsicum and rice mixture into the prepared baking dish, and press the mixture down with the back of a spoon. Bake for 35–40 minutes, or until the mixture begins to brown lightly. Remove from the oven and leave to cool for 15 minutes before slicing into wedges. Serve warm.

NUTRITION PER SERVE: *Protein 15 g; Fat 30 g; Carbohydrate 50 g; Dietary Fibre 2 g; Cholesterol 120 mg; 2200 kJ (525 cal)*

*Capsicum Herb Rice Cake (top) with Salmon and Fennel Salad*

## Salmon and Fennel Salad

*Preparation time:*
15 minutes
*Total cooking time:*
Nil
*Serves 4*

***Dressing***
*2 teaspoons Dijon mustard*
*1 teaspoon caster sugar*
*1/2 cup (125 ml/4 fl oz) olive oil*
*2 tablespoons lemon juice*

*2 fennel bulbs, thinly sliced*
*150 g (5 oz) sliced smoked salmon, cut into strips*
*2 tablespoons chopped chives*
*1 tablespoon chopped fennel fronds*
*rocket leaves, to serve*

**1. To make Dressing:** Whisk the mustard, sugar, olive oil and lemon juice in a large bowl until combined.
**2.** Add the fennel, salmon, chives and fennel fronds to the Dressing. Season with salt and pepper and toss gently. Serve immediately with the rocket leaves.

NUTRITION PER SERVE: *Protein 10 g; Fat 30 g; Carbohydrate 4 g; Dietary Fibre 3 g; Cholesterol 20 mg; 1415 kJ (335 cal)*

## Rack of Lamb with Coriander Stuffing

*Preparation time:*
25 minutes
*Total cooking time:*
50 minutes
*Serves 4*

*2 tablespoons oil*
*1 onion, chopped*
*100 g (3 1/4 oz) English spinach leaves, shredded*
*2 cloves garlic, crushed*
*2 teaspoons grated fresh ginger*
*1/2 cup (25 g/3/4 oz) chopped coriander*
*2 teaspoons grated lime rind*
*1/2 cup (40 g/1 1/4 oz) fresh breadcrumbs*
*2 x 6 cutlet racks of lamb*
*1 tablespoon sweet chilli sauce*
*2 teaspoons lime juice*
*spicy mango chutney, to serve*

**1.** Preheat the oven to very hot 230°C (450°F/Gas 8). Heat half the oil in a pan, add the onion and stir until it is translucent. Add the shredded spinach, garlic and ginger, and stir until the spinach has just wilted. Remove from the heat and allow to cool. Squeeze out any excess liquid and transfer the spinach to a bowl. Add the coriander, lime rind and fresh breadcrumbs, and mix well.

**2.** Trim the lamb racks of any excess fat. Using a sharp knife, separate the meat from the bones at the centre of each rack along the bone to form a small pocket. Cover the tops of the bones with foil. Using the end of a teaspoon, press the spinach mixture firmly into the lamb pockets. Rub a little salt and freshly ground black pepper over the lamb. Place the lamb on a wire rack in a baking dish, and brush with the combined sweet chilli sauce, lime juice and remaining oil.

**3.** Bake for 10 minutes, then reduce the heat to moderately hot 200°C (400°F/Gas 6). Bake for a further 30 minutes for a medium result. Baste the lamb once or twice during cooking. Stand the racks for 5 minutes before slicing and serving with the spicy mango chutney.

NUTRITION PER SERVE:
*Protein 25 g; Fat 30 g; Carbohydrate 15 g; Dietary Fibre 3 g; Cholesterol 85 mg; 1805 kJ (430 cal)*

**Note:** The lamb may be stuffed up to two hours ahead and refrigerated until needed. Return to room temperature before baking.

*Rack of Lamb with Coriander Stuffing*

*1 Mix the coriander, lime rind and breadcrumbs with the spinach mixture.*

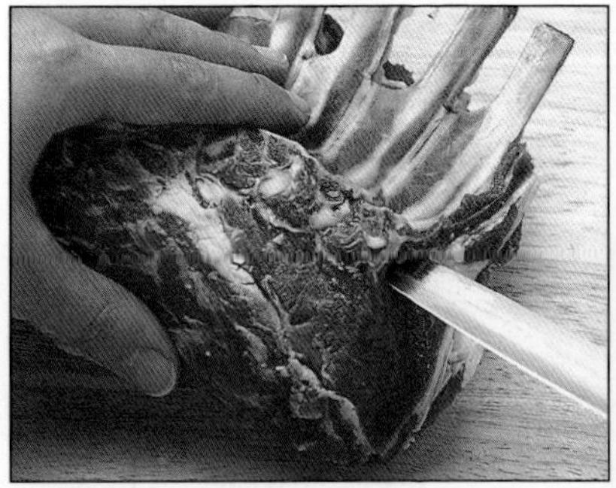

*2 Separate the meat from the bones to form a small pocket.*

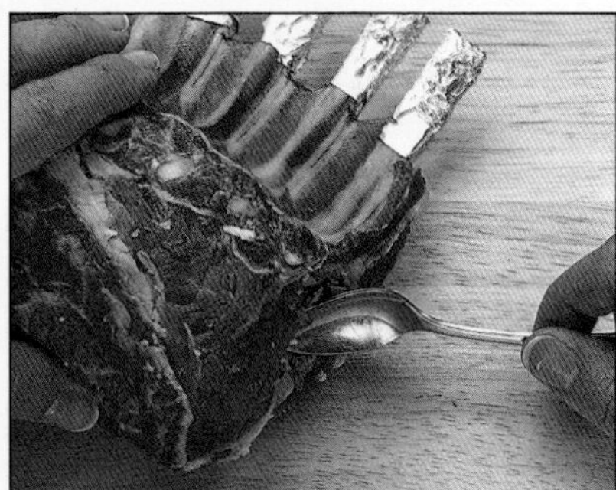

*3 Cover the bones with foil and press the spinach mixture firmly into the pocket.*

*4 Brush the lamb with the combined sweet chilli sauce, lime juice and oil.*

## Rosemary Roasted Chicken with Vegetables

*Preparation time:* 20 minutes
*Total cooking time:* 1 hour 15 minutes
*Serves 4*

*1 large chicken, cut into 8 pieces (you can ask the poultry shop to do this)*
*4 large parsnips, cut into chunks*
*4 pontiac potatoes, cut into chunks*
*1 red capsicum, cut into chunks*
*2 tablespoons olive oil*
*1 bulb of garlic, cloves separated but not peeled*
*1 tablespoon rosemary leaves*
*2 teaspoons thyme leaves*
*3 small sprigs rosemary, to garnish*
*1 lemon, cut into wedges, to serve*

**1.** Preheat the oven to hot 220°C (425°F/Gas 7). Put the chicken pieces and parsnip in a large baking dish. Bring a pan of salted water to the boil. Drop the potato chunks into the boiling water, cook for 5 minutes then drain completely. Add to the baking dish along with the capsicum chunks.
**2.** Drizzle the olive oil over the chicken and vegetables, and scatter the cloves of garlic, rosemary leaves, thyme and a little salt over the top. Bake for about 1 hour 10 minutes, turning the chicken and vegetables every 20 minutes or so. When cooked, the vegetables will be tender with crispy edges, and the chicken will be golden. Test the chicken by pricking it with a sharp knife. The juices will be clear when cooked.
**3.** Arrange the chicken and vegetables on a large warm serving platter, place the rosemary sprigs on top and scatter the lemon wedges around.

NUTRITION PER SERVE:
*Protein 40 g; Fat 20 g; Carbohydrate 30 g; Dietary Fibre 7 g; Cholesterol 110 mg; 1805 kJ (430 cal)*

**Note:** Tell your guests to squeeze the cloves of garlic out of the skins and onto the chicken and vegetables.
**Variation:** Omit the chicken to make a delicious warm salad. Drizzle the salad with a little olive oil and balsamic vinegar.

*Rosemary Roasted Chicken with Vegetables (top) with Herb Spaghetti*

## Herb Spaghetti

*Preparation time:* 20 minutes
*Total cooking time:* 15 minutes
*Serves 4*

*1/4 cup (20 g/3/4 oz) fresh breadcrumbs*
*500 g (1 lb) spaghetti*
*3 tablespoons olive oil*
*2 cloves garlic, diced*
*1 cup (30 g/1 oz) chopped herbs (basil, coriander, parsley)*
*4 tomatoes, chopped*
*1/4 cup (30 g/1 oz) chopped walnuts*
*1/4 cup (25 g/3/4 oz) grated Parmesan*

**1.** Put the breadcrumbs under a medium grill for a few seconds, or until golden.
**2.** Cook the pasta in boiling water until tender, then drain.
**3.** Heat 2 tablespoons of the olive oil in a large frying pan and cook the garlic until soft. Add the remaining oil and the herbs, tomato, walnuts and Parmesan, reserving a little to serve. Add the pasta and toss for 1–2 minutes. Top with the breadcrumbs and reserved Parmesan.

NUTRITION PER SERVE:
*Protein 20 g; Fat 25 g; Carbohydrate 95 g; Dietary Fibre 9 g; Cholesterol 6 mg; 2825 kJ (620 cal)*

## Chargrilled Tuna and Noodle Salad

*Preparation time:*
30 minutes +
2 hours marinating
*Total cooking time:*
20 minutes
*Serves 6*

*6 tuna steaks*
*1/2 cup (125 ml/4 fl oz) lime juice*
*200 g (6 1/2 oz) dried thin egg noodles*
*2 teaspoons sesame oil*
*90 g (3 oz) snow peas, cut into thin strips*
*1 small red capsicum, cut into thin strips*
*1 small carrot, cut into thin strips*
*2 spring onions, cut into long thin strips*
*1 green and 1 red chilli, cut into thin strips*
*1/4 cup (15 g/1/2 oz) coriander leaves, coarsely shredded*
*3 cm (1 1/4 inch) piece fresh ginger, cut into thin strips*

***Lemon Grass Dressing***
*1 stem lemon grass, white part only, finely chopped*
*1 tablespoon chopped coriander roots and stems*
*1 clove garlic, crushed*
*3 teaspoons grated lime rind*
*2 tablespoons lime juice*
*3 teaspoons fish sauce*
*1 cup (250 ml/8 fl oz) coconut milk*

**1.** Pat the tuna dry with paper towels. Place in a bowl, drizzle with the lime juice and sprinkle with salt and pepper. Cover and refrigerate for up to 2 hours.
**2.** Cook the noodles in boiling water until tender. Rinse, drain and cut into shorter lengths. Toss the noodles in the sesame oil, add the snow peas, capsicum, carrot, onion, chilli, coriander and ginger.
**3. To make Lemon Grass Dressing:** Blend or process the lemon grass, coriander, garlic, lime rind, juice, fish sauce and coconut milk until smooth. The dressing separates on standing so pour into a screw-top jar and shake well before serving.
**4.** Cook the tuna on a preheated barbecue grill plate or in a chargrill pan, basting with any remaining lime juice, for 2–3 minutes on each side—tuna becomes dry and tough if it is overcooked. Break the tuna into pieces and gently toss with the salad. Drizzle with the Lemon Grass Dressing.

NUTRITION PER SERVE:
*Protein 45 g; Fat 15 g; Carbohydrate 25 g; Dietary Fibre 2 g; Cholesterol 85 mg; 1755 kJ (415 cal)*

## Asparagus with Basil Tomatoes

*Preparation time:*
20 minutes
*Total cooking time:*
5 minutes
*Serves 4*

*4 egg tomatoes, peeled*
*300 g (10 oz) asparagus*
*50 g (1 3/4 oz) butter*
*1 clove garlic, crushed*
*1/2 teaspoon sugar*
*2 tablespoons dry white wine*
*1 tablespoon shredded basil*
*1/2 cup (50 g/1 3/4 oz) grated Parmesan*

**1.** Cut each tomato into 4 wedges and remove the seeds. Cook the asparagus in boiling water for 2 minutes, or until just tender. Drain, cover and keep warm.
**2.** Melt the butter in a pan, add the garlic, tomato, sugar and wine and toss over high heat for 45 seconds. Season and add the basil.
**3.** Spoon the tomato mixture over the asparagus and top with the grated Parmesan. Serve immediately.

NUTRITION PER SERVE:
*Protein 8 g; Fat 15 g; Carbohydrate 4 g; Dietary Fibre 3 g; Cholesterol 45 mg; 770 kJ (185 cal)*

*Chargrilled Tuna and Noodle Salad (top) with Asparagus with Basil Tomatoes*

## Herbed Naan Bread

*Preparation time:*
35 minutes + rising
*Total cooking time:*
20 minutes
*Serves 4*

*1 packet naan bread mix*
*1/2 cup (30 g/1 oz) mixed chopped herbs (coriander, parsley, chives)*
*2 tablespoons mango chutney*
*1/2 cup (90 g/3 oz) cooked and finely diced pumpkin*
*1/2 cup (90 g/3 oz) cooked and finely diced sweet potato*
*1/2 cup (90 g/3 oz) cooked peas*
*1 teaspoon curry powder*
*1/2 teaspoon garam masala*
*1 teaspoon crushed fennel seeds*
*1/4 teaspoon chilli powder*
*1 egg, lightly beaten*

**1.** Prepare the naan bread according to the instructions up to the risen stage.
**2.** Combine the herbs, chutney, vegetables, curry powder, garam masala, fennel seeds and chilli powder in a bowl. Preheat the oven to moderately hot 200°C (400°F/Gas 6).
**3.** Divide the dough into 4 pieces and roll each out to a 15 cm (6 inch) circle. Spread a quarter of the filling on half of each piece, fold over and seal the edges with a little of the egg. Brush the top with the remaining egg. Place on an oven tray and bake for 20 minutes.

NUTRITION PER SERVE:
*Protein 15 g; Fat 15 g; Carbohydrate 70 g; Dietary Fibre 3 g; Cholesterol 45 mg; 1865 kJ (445 cal)*

## Baked Stuffed Mushrooms

*Preparation time:*
20 minutes
*Total cooking time:*
20 minutes
*Serves 4*

*16 large flat mushrooms*
*60 g (2 oz) butter*
*1 clove garlic, crushed*
*1/2 cup (125 g/4 oz) ricotta cheese*
*75 g (2 1/2 oz) goats cheese, chopped*
*1 tablespoon chopped chives*
*2 teaspoons chopped thyme*

**1.** Preheat the oven to moderate 180°C (350°F/Gas 4). Brush a baking tray with melted butter or oil. Wipe the mushrooms gently with a soft damp cloth to remove any excess dirt. Remove the mushroom stalks from the caps. Melt the butter in a small pan, add the garlic and cook for 1 minute, or until golden. Brush the inside of the mushroom caps lightly with half of the garlic butter.
**2.** Combine the ricotta, goats cheese, chives and thyme in a small bowl, and season with black pepper. Spread the filling on the flat side of half of the mushrooms and top with the remaining mushrooms.
**3.** Place the stuffed mushrooms on a baking tray and brush the tops with the remaining garlic butter. Bake for 15 minutes, or until the mushrooms are tender and cooked. Serve immediately.

NUTRITION PER SERVE:
*Protein 10 g; Fat 20 g; Carbohydrate 2 g; Dietary Fibre 3 g; Cholesterol 65 mg; 970 kJ (230 cal)*

**Note:** Always clean mushrooms by wiping them with a soft damp cloth. Do not immerse them in water or they will be soggy and lose their flavour.

*Herbed Naan Bread (top) with Baked Stuffed Mushrooms*

# After-dinner Herbs

You can never have too much of a good thing, so why should you leave herbs behind with the main course? Dare to be different with these delicious sweet treats.

## Lavender Ice Cream

Wash and dry 8 stems of English lavender. Put in a pan with 2 1/2 cups (600 ml/20 fl oz) thick cream and 1 small piece of lemon rind. Heat the mixture until almost boiling. Stir in 2/3 cup (160 g/5 1/4 oz) sugar until dissolved. Strain through a fine sieve. Pour onto 4 whisked egg yolks and beat. (If it does not thicken immediately, return to the heat over a double boiler and thicken gently.) When the mixture is thick enough to coat the back of a spoon, pour it into a chilled baking dish to cool. With the freezer at its lowest setting, freeze the mixture until frozen around the edge (but not in the middle). Beat until smooth. Refreeze and repeat twice when the mixture is half frozen. *Serves 6–8*

NUTRITION PER SERVE (8): *Protein 3 g; Fat 30 g; Carbohydrate 20 g; Dietary Fibre 0 g; Cholesterol 175 mg; 1520 kJ (360 cal)*

**Note:** If the lavender is in full flower, use less, or the ice cream will taste too strong.

## Spearmint Citrus Sorbet

Place 1 1/2 cups (375 g/12 oz) caster sugar, 2 cups (50 g/1 3/4 oz) spearmint leaves and 3 cups (750 ml/24 fl oz) water in a pan. Bring to the boil then simmer for 30 minutes. Pour the liquid through a strainer and discard the spearmint leaves. Add 3/4 cup (185 ml/6 fl oz) lemon or grapefruit

juice, $1^1/4$ cups (315 ml/ 10 fl oz) orange juice and $^1/2$ cup (125 ml/ 4 fl oz) dry white wine, and stir. Pour into a plastic container and, once cool, stir in $^1/2$ cup (15 g/$^1/2$ oz) finely sliced spearmint. Freeze until the sorbet is just firm. Place in a food processor and process until smooth. Return to the freezer and freeze overnight, or until firm. Allow the sorbet to soften slightly before scooping out. Garnish with a slice of citrus and a sprig of spearmint. *Serves 6–8*

NUTRITION PER SERVE (8): *Protein 0 g; Fat 0 g; Carbohydrate 50 g; Dietary Fibre 0 g; Cholesterol 0 mg; 875 kJ (210 cal)*

## Rosemary Biscotti

Preheat the oven to moderately hot 200°C (400°F/Gas 6). Combine 3 cups (375 g/ 12 oz) plain flour, $^3/4$ cup (185 g/6 oz) caster sugar, 1 teaspoon baking powder, $^1/4$ teaspoon salt, 125 g (4 oz) chilled butter, 1 tablespoon finely chopped rosemary leaves, 2 teaspoons finely grated lemon rind and $1^1/4$ cups (150 g/5 oz) roughly chopped hazelnuts in a food processor. Process until thoroughly mixed. Add 3 tablespoons lemon juice, 2 lightly whisked eggs, $^1/2$ teaspoon vanilla essence and 1 teaspoon rose water. Blend until the mixture forms a dough. (This can all be done by hand in a mixing bowl.) Divide the mixture into 4 and roll into log shapes 3 cm ($1^1/4$ inches) wide. Place on greased baking trays and bake for 20 minutes. Reduce the oven to moderate 180°C (350°F/Gas 4). Allow to cool slightly before slicing each log into 1 cm ($^1/2$ inch) thick diagonal slices. Spread out on the baking trays and return to the oven for a further 5–8 minutes. Cool on wire racks. *Makes about 60*

NUTRITION PER BISCUIT: *Protein 1 g; Fat 3 g; Carbohydrate 8 g; Dietary Fibre 0 g; Cholesterol 10 mg; 280 kJ (65 cal)*

*Left to right: Lavender Ice Cream; Spearmint Citrus Sorbet; Rosemary Biscotti*

# Index